What shines through Murdo M  p in the Highlands, to his successf with a devastating diagnosis of ter ong personal Christian faith has su nily, even in the darkest times. Murd ved, and will prove an inspiration to

.aser

MSP for Mid-Scotland and Fife

For a man who dealt with Classic cars, this is 'classic' Murdo! Profound and poignant, as we see the Lord's plans and purposes for his life unfold before our eyes. My first contact with Murdo was through the Motor trade when I ran a car-hire business in Benbecula. Partnering with him now in the business of winning souls for our Saviour in Stirling is far better. I am privileged to know the man and call him my friend.

Iain MacAskill
Pastor, Stirling Free Church of Scotland, Stirling

I have had the privilege of having Murdo Murchison as a close friend for the best part of forty years. He has always been blessed with the gift of vision. When others were paralysed and consumed by problems he was always motivated by possibilities. If ever there was a person who lived out the verse, 'For to me, to live is Christ, to die is gain' it is Murdo. The chapters of this book reveal a mind which sees the extraordinary in the ordinary. It is fitting that Murdo's main hobby was flying. His view of the world was always from a height which enabled him to enjoy the past with a degree of healthy nostalgia but which also give him an optimistic view of the future. In this book we see that Murdo, bravely and honestly, writing out of a context of terminal illness, sees that the future is not dark but is as bright as the promises of God. Murdo has been consistent in sickness and in health. His motivation to speak about the gospel was not in the slightest way affected by his prognosis. He was always a man who 'preached as never sure to preach again, and as a dying man to dying men.' The hero of this book is not the wee boy, raised in Kyle of Lochalsh, it's not the highly successful car salesman and it's not even the man who is not wasting his cancer. The dominant figure is Jesus Christ, the same, yesterday, today and forever.'

David Meredith
Mission Director, Free Church of Scotland

An entertaining and inspirational read.

George Mackenzie
Managing Director, Donald Mackenzie Ltd.

Murdo Murchison is a friend. So I feel I can say what I feel after reading his book! Murdo is not a writer, he is a second hand car salesmen. At least he was until he was diagnosed with serious brain cancer and now lo and behold he has become a writer – and a good one at that! I had suggested to him when I heard of his illness that he should start blogging – because he had some really interesting stories to tell. This wee book is the result of that. It's a wee gem! It's not the doom and gloom sombre reflection you might expect. Nor does it trivialise or try to humourise what are the most serious aspects of life and death. If you are interested in the Highlands, cars, family, planes, humanity, Christianity and life and death – you will love *One Good Owner*. It is well written, clear, interesting, real, sad, joyful, full of life and full of hope. Inspiring for Christians and non-Christians alike!

David Robertson
Minister, St Peter's Free Church, Dundee

The author and I, kinsmen and brothers, have been reflecting on life, like a couple of old Highlanders, for as long as I can remember. As a wee boy, I looked up to 'Murdo Kyle', or 'Mountain Murdo'. Still do. In the beginning, age mattered, and so it was that he, being just a few months older, was charged, in the summer of 1971, with the responsibility of escorting me, not yet in Secondary School, across the Minch, to a Free Church Camp in Lewis. It was a momentous trip. It was there that I first began to wrestle with some of the questions that really matter in life. Age still matters – as does the question of time. Murdo, of course, was never short of questions. He had, and still has, the kind of restless assuredness about him which I have found, and, perhaps through this book, others will continue to find, both challenging and engaging. I commend to you Murdo's story, it is one which I am honoured to say has been entwined with my own. More than that I commend to you Murdo's Lord, to Whom we may bring our questions, and in Whom we find meaning and purpose, and life in all its fullness.

Kenneth Ian MacKenzie D.L.
Minister of The Parish of Braemar and Crathie and
Domestic Chaplain to Her Majesty The Queen in Scotland

From wandering the heather-clad hills near Kyle, to lying in the cancer unit at the Western in Edinburgh, Murdo tells his story with warmth and ease. It's the story of ordinary confidence in an uncertain world. On one hand, I find it easy to relate to Murdo's journey, of busyness, activity and work. Like me, I am sure others are guilty of getting caught up in the temporal things of here and now even as Christians. But for those of us who like stability and control, Murdo's writing reminds us of the uncertainty and unpredictability that no amount of 21st century comfort can combat. Murdo's testimony encourages me greatly to store up treasures of permanent value – it won't be in vain because it is ultimately all that matters on both sides of death.

Kate Forbes MSP
Skye, Lochaber and Badenoch

ONE GOOD OWNER

God is in the Driving Seat

MURDO MURCHISON

CHRISTIAN
FOCUS

Copyright © Murdo Murchison 2017
Paperback ISBN: 978-1-5271-0029-9
Epub ISBN: 978-1-5271-0056-5
Mobi ISBN: 978-1-5271-0057-2

Published in 2017
by Christian Focus Publications Ltd,
Geanies House, Fearn, Ross-shire,
IV20 1TW, Scotland, U.K.
www.christianfocus.com

Cover design by Daniel van Straaten

Printed and bound by
Bell and Bain, Glasgow

MIX
Paper from responsible sources
FSC® C007785
www.fsc.org

We are grateful to John Reid for the cover photo.

CONTENTS

Introduction

In mid August 2016, supposing you had told me that in a few months' time I would have written a book, some laughter would have followed! My life till then had been fairly active and very much biased towards practical activities. On 30th August, Margaret, who trained as a nurse, was sure I had died following a massive seizure. From then on, following partial and temporary recovery, life was to be very different. No longer a fit, young, active fifty-eight-year-old but suddenly and whether I like it or not, effectively an old man!

As I write seven months on, having been given just three months to live, last December brain surgery saved my life, giving me a year or maybe longer, humanly speaking. You may well ask why did God not just take me to heaven at 2 am on 30th August, 2016? In trying to answer, three things come to mind as I speculate in the context of the biblical truth that the ways of our sovereign, all-knowing God are past finding out!

Firstly: For some time my prayer, almost daily had been, 'Please God, while I am grateful for so many material blessings, give me deep and meaningful spiritual blessing, a longing similar to the great Apostle Paul: *That I may know him and the power of his resurrection.*' Since the seizure I have had more of a peace within which I put down largely to the prayers of people worldwide. It simply is not in my nature to be at peace when ill. With time to reflect and pray, although much is still a mystery, God has helped me just as He promises. I have learned one lesson about prayer ... be careful what you pray for!

Secondly: There was some fairly complex but mundane business which needed to be sorted out and this work is ongoing. It is a privilege to be able to tidy up my secular affairs and make sure that the family are as secure as possible.

Thirdly: Spreading the gospel through blogging and various forms of social media may have been a totally alien concept pre-tumour, but now seems to be an important tool for evangelism so I am encouraging others to use it. Church planting and preaching, which was part of my previous life, is extremely effective, but social media and this book have a different type of reach, which should not be underestimated. God has given me a great opportunity and He could give further opportunities ... there is no greater privilege this side of heaven than to spread the Good News. New ways of presenting the gospel emerge all the time.

Murdo Murchison before his illness

A Bad Diagnosis

On the 30th of August my life changed completely when, at 2.30 in the morning, I had a massive seizure. The family thought I had died, but I came back to consciousness in the ambulance on the way to Larbert Hospital. It was clear to the hospital that heart, blood pressure etc., were all textbook so within six hours I had the result of a CT scan showing a two centimetre tumour between the sensory cortex and the motor cortex of the brain.

The coming days and indeed weeks were a bit of a blur as I adjusted to anti-seizure drugs and came to realize that my future would be very different. On the 20th of September I was told that brain surgery would most likely impair motor function. The blunt diagnosis was that depending on tumour growth my life expectancy could range from three to twenty years.

No more driving, cycling, hill walking, flying light aircraft and working machinery for me. Forced retirement from running a thriving car business was necessary. Despite this, I have been able to hang on to a property firm comprising of a dozen or so let units.

The question people ask is: How does this terrible experience fit in with your much talked about faith? Do you still have faith? The answer to that question is a resounding YES. Despite that affirmation, when I regained consciousness on the way to Larbert Hospital, I was pretty scared and confused. There seemed to be no comfort and my great question was, where is God? – The great God of all comfort who works all things for the good of His people.

Brought up to know and read the Bible, having been both a lay preacher and more recently a church planter, the one thing I could and indeed can latch on to is the amazing life of Jesus Christ which has me believing that He died for my sins on the cross and rose victorious from the dead. Many times through life I had listened to various other theories but could not and indeed cannot find better than Jesus Christ and the glorious, unique gospel.

That's a pretty poor kind of theoretical faith I hear you say, and I agree. Surely there is more than that at the end of a life spent promoting a book full of amazing promises.

Cards, e-mails, letters, phone calls, Facebook messages and visits, all with pledges of prayer, flooded in and in early September, gradually a deep, inexplicable peace took over. Despite this, for reasons which I just cannot explain, I have not been able to pray much myself but it feels as though I sit on a cushion of prayer ... a very comfortable place to be. God does answer prayer. People tell me that despite having little or even no faith they are praying and that really moves me!

With the grim reality of a shortened life kicking in and multiple seizures most days, I am unable to live the way I had hoped to for the next twenty years. My fitness level is still pretty good for a fifty-eight-year-old, but the seizures exhaust me each day and my left side sensory function is declining. I have become increasingly frustrated, not able to tie shoes and buttons, cutting my face shaving, dropping things. Getting angry with myself is all part of it.

The great Apostle Paul talks of being sorrowful yet always rejoicing and I now know exactly what he means. The Bible talks of the outward man fading away but being renewed in the inner man. I can relate very well to that great concept.

Whatever your philosophy in life, try reading the Bible. It's just amazing how God's Word explains the problems of life and tells us how to face up to death itself with a smile!

Today at a meeting with the consultant surgeon it became very clear that the tumour had doubled in size and the diagnosis is now that growth is very aggressive. An operation is scheduled on 5th December and will give me some extra months if successful.

Please pray for me at this difficult time, also for Margaret and the family. I want to have the same peace as I had back in early September.

'A Picture can say a Thousand Words'

When I collapsed with a massive seizure, the family thought I had gone to my Maker. Life pre-seizure was very different to post seizure. My old life included running a couple of businesses, preaching, church planting in Stirling, flying light aircraft and property development. As the old people would have said, 'If I am spared' my life will be very different but I hope, God willing, to make the most of the time I have left.

Aged nine or ten, there was nothing I liked more than wandering the hills between Kyle and Balmacara. When you crossed Main Street, Kyle, you were in a different, magnificent, heather-clad world with small burns, ponds and lochs. The views are fantastic from Beinn na

Caillich, on top of which a Norwegian princess was buried. The world famous Cuillins are to the West and to the North the Bealach na Bà has the highest road in Britain. The colours overhead can be seen from miles away as they change with the weather. I still remember the boats as they came and went in Lochalsh and the Sound of Raasay at varying speeds. Dun Caan, an ancient volcano on the Island of Raasay, stood out from every angle.

That was my world. My magical world. The one I escaped to when I left the much hated, loathed, and detested school. In the hills you seldom saw anybody, even after hours of wandering. The further away I got, the happier I became. My habit was to raid the biscuit tin and hope that my spoil would not melt too much as I walked!

Weather never mattered that much, it was just the sense of freedom. In the photograph, I'm wearing two jerseys which reminds me that this was a cold spring day with the heather in bloom. In these times, short trousers were very much a requirement in school and I quite liked them. The barber who cut my hair had recently chased me for mucking about with my friends while waiting for a haircut on a Saturday morning. The old rascal managed to get his own back as you can see! Rumour had it that he had been an Army Barber at the time of World War II. Could the haircut amount to cruelty to children?

Murdo on a hill. The Cuillins of Skye are in the background and the dreaded Kyle School is to the left.

From my world of mountains and lochs I would look down on the village of Kyle where I had a sense of the insignificance and smallness of all the people living their lives down below. When I escaped that world there was a strong sense of the awesome sovereign God who created this vast world which He controls and governs. It was inconceivable, even to a small boy, that it had randomly evolved. But I have to confess that God, at that time, was even more real to me than He is nearly fifty years later … perhaps I have not wandered these hills of home enough in adult life?

Wetting the Head

I was born in April 1958 and as there had not been a birth in the Kyle Murchison family since my dad in 1925, great rejoicing followed my arrival. My dad even brought a bottle of

Murdo as a baby

whisky for the staff at the garage to share; from a twenty-first century perspective this seems quite extraordinary when you consider the fact that some of these men would have been driving the school bus, the ambulance, as well as working machinery.

Probably, in line with every other country garage, there was little or no consideration to health and safety. I think of the conditions I worked in as a boy: oily floors, a large waste oil heater burned red hot in the middle of the workshop as we sprayed cars with highly flammable cellulose paint, the oxy acetylene welder had leaking hoses, jacks lost hydraulic pressure and general junk was piled up around the place. Water poured in on electrical fittings and you regularly got a 240 volt hair-raising shock off the battered hand lamps working below cars down the pit!

One Saturday morning my young brother Ian was lighting the dirty, smelly but very effective waste oil heater using paraffin and a newspaper with no apparent success. (On a good day, it burned red hot right up the flume.) Suddenly there was a loud explosion as the primitive apparatus came to life. His hair and nylon –

YES nylon – boiler suit burned ferociously. We immediately forced him to the floor, rolled him around and threw water at his burning hair. From the state of his boiler suit and loss of hair he was fortunate to survive. It is remarkable that the instinct to somehow quench the fire and save his life kicked in. Not convinced I would be just as fast thinking these days. A good haircut later and the only evidence of his near-death experience was lack of eyebrows as well as some inflammation on his neck and forehead. He certainly had a wetting of the head that day ... and maybe even a baptism of fire!

I am often the first to complain about health and safety gone mad and the high cost of it but, then again, can a price be put on life? The 'good old days' in many ways were not so good. The only concession to health and safety at the garage in Kyle was a faded laminated copy of the 'Factories Act 1960' hanging proudly on the wall. I used to wonder, 'Why is that irrelevant rubbish taking up space?' My conclusion nowadays, perhaps slightly reluctantly, is that despite the expense of rigorous health and safety, the wellbeing of people does need to be emphasised in a balanced and meaningful manner. In fact, to go further and maybe even irk some people, is it not better to see lives saved rather than have too lax an attitude leading ultimately to unnecessary deaths?

From a Christian standpoint each human being is uniquely and wonderfully made in the image of the great Creator God, therefore no price can be too high to protect life in the workplace. As the truly amazing Apostle Paul reminded the debaters of Athens long ago: 'we are indeed his offspring'.

Tear-away Tot!

If you are into cars you will be horrified to read about the destruction of a rare classic! At the age of four I was very much the centre of attention within the family and was given the freedom to do whatever I liked. If not … watch out, there would be a horrendous tantrum.

At the side of the family home sat a car described as 'Art Deco on wheels'. It was a 1941 Buick Century convertible and I considered it to be a fun car to play in with my little friends. My grandfather Murdo had a liking for big American cars but, by the time I was around, had given up driving. My dad told me that, by pre-school age, I had succeeded in completely wrecking the Buick; indeed that the scrap man ended up lifting it.

Murdo on his bike

I will confess to putting stones in the petrol tank, breaking switches and ripping the hood. Other than that I simply do not remember 'wrecking it'. Are you seriously telling me that a four-year-old had that ability? Personally, I blame the parents!

I hope that all the sensitive classic car lovers will be able to sleep tonight after reading this horrendous tale of woe! The one I wrecked was yellow with black wings and had brown leather. We're not even going to think about how much it would be worth today!

To make a more serious point the clear message of the first book of the Bible is that we are all the children of Adam and Eve and that nobody has to teach us how to do wrong. The Bible constantly points us to the remedy, the cross of Jesus which reconciles us to God through His death and resurrection.

That early instinct to destroy leads me to think about how a loving God accepts me. He willingly takes the punishment for my past and future misdemeanours provided I believe and accept that the sacrifice of Jesus on the cross was for my sins. He can do it for you as well! That is the message of the Bible. It's SO SIMPLE! Why do many Christian churches complicate it?

Finding myself now on the final bend before the home straight for heaven I am totally confident that the cross of Jesus has reconciled me to my Maker.

There again a sovereign God is also the God of miracles! He could decide to give me more time in this lower world.

Murchison Monument

Murchison Monument

Growing up I was very much aware that there was a strong connection between my grandfather and the Murchison Monument which sits between Kyle and Balmacara, right in the middle of Lochalsh. On our sideboard at A'Chomraich (our home in Kyle) sat a rose bowl presented to my grandfather, also named Murdo Murchison, for his contribution in restoring the monument when struck by lightning in 1927 and again in 1928. My father, Finlay, as a four-year-old circa 1929, put the newspaper and coinage of the day into the new foundation. In our family, it was simply known as 'the monument' as if no other monument existed!

On a Saturday afternoon, a good walk was to go along the Balmacara footpath before the coast road was built between Balmacara and Kyle in 1968. As a young man working in the family garage, when test driving cars following repair, I would take them to 'the monument' and back to Kyle. The base of the silver rose bowl is distorted. This is probably due to it being thrown around by me and my siblings!

Sir Roderick Murchison, the erector of the monument, explorer, pioneering-geologist and founder of the Royal Geographical Society, visited his kinsfolk – my great-great-grandfather – circa 1850 and was appalled by the turf-roofed family home. He writes about this in one of his books. Despite a stern conversation about moving into the nineteenth century a friendship continued down the generations and the widow of Roderick Murchison's grand-nephew Kenneth, Lady Mary Murchison, stayed with my family in Kyle a couple of times when I was small.

The prominent granite monument was in memory of Colonel Donald Murchison, Sir Roderick's great-grand uncle, who was born in Bundaloch near Dornie in 1687. In 1715, when the Earl of Seaforth conscripted 3000 of his tenants to join the Stuart Standard, Donald was made his Lieutenant at the age of just twenty-eight. For the next twelve years with multiple adventures he fiercely protected the Earl of Seaforth's interests throughout the Highlands.

Sir Roderick organised a huge ceremony on completion of the structure in 1863. The future King Edward VII attended along with some officers from the Atlantic fleet which then had boats in Lochalsh, Edward at that time serving as a midshipman.

There is a painting that features my ancestor Donald Murchison, wearing a breastplate under his jacket. He was defying the law on behalf of the Jacobite Earl of Seaforth, exiled in Paris after the defeat of the Old Pretender's army at the Battle of Sheriffmuir in 1715. The painting has the Earl's tenants hiding from the redcoats across the loch. Providence has me living in more civilized times than my distant ancestor! Legend has it that he was caught on one of his return trips from France and imprisoned in the Tower of London, eventually receiving a pardon from George I.

By the time Donald was aged forty the Earl of Seaforth was back from exile and Donald, still unmarried, quite reasonably expected to be gifted an Estate – perhaps Lochalsh or Lochcarron; instead he was offered a farm at Bundaloch. Sickened, hurt and furious he took to his bed. Seaforth, realizing his mistake and meanness, came to ask forgiveness as Donald lay dying but Donald declared 'God may forgive you but I will not.' My advice to him were it possible to have met him would have come from Psalm 146 verse 3:

> *Put not your trust in princes, nor in the son of man, in whom there is no help.*

To conclude, was Donald a villain, or a hero? Well, nobody could deny the fact that he was a clever battle strategist: gallant, tough, and loyal. He truly lived up to the family crest, *Impavido Pectore* ('With undaunted heart').

London 1966 ... Not the World Cup!

One fine spring day my dad Finlay got it into his mind that it would be a good idea to have a camper van for holidays and appropriately for a Morris dealer found a Morris J2 in London for sale. He decided it would be a good idea to take me with him at the age of eight. Permission to be off school for a week was readily granted on the basis that I would return with a full report of the wonderful sites visited.

We took the evening train from Kyle then following some Edinburgh visits took one of the famous steam trains to London, similar to the Flying Scotsman. This, however, was totally lost on me having seen many smelly old steam trains trundle into Kyle. Diesel, even to a young boy, seemed like a much better, cleaner, idea. My dad put me on board the steam train then went off to make phone calls. The whistle went so I alerted the guard explaining that my dad had not turned up. Just as I stepped back on the platform he appeared and we got on board, a bad start as I was in tears wondering what would have happened to me. My dad, on the other hand, normally very sympathetic when disaster struck, dismissed it as trivial … he would have caught up with me at the next station!

On arrival in London we went round some of the sites and to be frank, despite good weather and some appreciation, I considered most of it to be pretty dull. What was so great about a boat trip down the murky Thames with horrible bridges and dull buildings on each side? Much nicer to go over the sea to Skye!

Buckingham Palace looked depressingly awful with too much bland tar all round it. The garage in Kyle would have made a better job of the gold paint on the gates! The guards did not appear to be much fun either.

St James's Park was very pleasant, but nothing compared to a wander round the Plock of Kyle with clear air and fantastic views. It was

Lord Byron who said, 'England thy beauties are tame and domestic to one who has roamed o'er the mountains afar.'

We queued for hours then gave up on the Crown Jewels. On seeing them many years later my thought was that I had been a wise eight-year-old to persuade my father to give up on the wait. As for Nelson's Column, the pigeons seemed dirty and the column was, after all, just a column.

On collecting the very nice green camper van, we set off up the almost empty four-year-old M1 Motorway and I thought it was great. The van sat nicely at sixty mph with an occasional fast car whizzing by. It impressed me even then thinking of the sheer volume of earth shifted to produce such a wide smooth road. As for the service areas, I thought they were just great. For sleeping, the camper worked very well with just two people. A different story with four or five!

On reaching Stafford, Dad went to see an old Albion long wheel base breakdown wagon which looked rubbish to me. He bought it and decided to take it eighty miles up the road and then return by train for the camper. With a worn engine it travelled at thirty mph going down to fifteen mph on the hills, dirty, noisy and filthy inside. The trip was now nose-diving! Despite Dad's obvious pleasure over his method of relaying the old breakdown home, I'd really had enough!

On the positive side, whether waiting for a train, on the train or sitting in a cafe, great conversation always took place with people we met and one of Dad's gifts, not really obvious at home, was to make interesting conversation with strangers. This gave me a very good impression of the English as a nation. There was of course much to be learned for a young boy just listening to the easy chat. I guess to use a cliché, in terms of education it comes under the 'university of life'.

A few days later we arrived home and by then I really did not want to see the old yellow breakdown wagon ever again, although it was around, quietly deteriorating, for many years.

So ... you may well be thinking, all this is quite interesting, but where is the biblical lesson woven into these stories? You may not like this, but I reported back that THE TRIP HAD BEEN WONDERFUL, the sites of London superb etc.,

etc. Maybe I should have been a political spin doctor instead of a mechanic!

The Bible tells us again and again from Genesis to Revelation that the human heart is sinful and that the answer to the problem lies in the Lord Jesus Christ, who in amazing love went to the cross and took our sins on Himself. We keep deceiving, lying and spinning stories ... not just me as a boy but all of us as adults! You may say, well it was harmless enough to put gloss on a report. The Bible, on the other hand, tells us of God who hates all types of wrongdoing and to find a just solution had to sacrifice His Son.

The greatness of the gospel lies in the fact that if we are trusting Jesus we have been justified by faith. No amount of good works can ever make us right with God. But on confessing our sins, He forgives! He has forgiven me for so much over the past fifty years. Have you asked for forgiveness? The gospel is for all of us! The slate can be wiped clean, the old account settled! Believe it or not, Psalm 103 even tells us that the sins of believers have been removed as far as east is from the west!

The Best 'Rags to Riches' Story Ever

Although I am not a reader, Margaret and, to a degree, the children are great readers. Were our rambling home a boat, with so many books on board, it would probably sink from the sheer weight of them in heavy sea!

What book (apart from the book of books) has influenced you the most in life? From quite a young age my dad would have us read a seventeenth-century book, *The Pilgrim's Progress* written by John Bunyan, a tinker from Bedford who wrote his masterpiece in jail. Sunday afternoon was the time set aside for that exercise. I can almost hear you saying, 'You poor soul, that sounds awful!' YOU WOULD BE WRONG THOUGH. It describes a fascinating journey from this world to the next and both gripped and caught the imagination of a nine or ten-year-old who had to read it to his younger siblings. Even today, give me *The Pilgrim's Progress* over the much-acclaimed Christian-based, *Lord of the Rings*, or, despite the spirit-world environment, the secular, Harry Potter series! Bunyan's work is just such a simple

Murdo with his dad and siblings

and direct allegory of the Bible itself. I found the characters with great names engaging, compelling and fascinating. Looking back on my life I see that I have interacted with types of people who reflect Bunyan's characters to some degree or other.

I simply love, or even love to hate, so many of the characters. I also, perhaps reluctantly, recognize a few of them within myself! 'Simple', 'Sloth' and 'Presumption' are great names for those who would not listen to Christian. How many 'Mr Worldly Wisemen' have I paid too much attention to? The honest answer is far too many. What about 'Flatterer'? The nine-year-old me should have paid more attention to that sneaky, subtle character. How about 'Mr Two Tongues'? Then there is the sad, well-expressed, martyrdom of 'Faithful' reminding us of the great power of evil which the believer wrestles against. Another memorable character is 'Mr Feeble Mind' – far too many like him have crossed my path in life.

Does this great quote tickle you? It does me!

'Mr Worldly Wiseman is an alien, Mr Legality is a cheat: As for his son Mr Civility, notwithstanding his simpering looks, is but a hypocrite.'

Cutting, simple and true where the message of the Bible is concerned.

The place names are, of course, brilliant. At one time I worked in the rather dull town of Slough and jokingly called it the 'Slough of Despond'. Even back in the eighties nobody in the secular world really understood that particular connection. However, everybody knows of 'Vanity Fair'. 'Doubting Castle' is a very real place to be reckoned with.

Charles H. Spurgeon, a great nineteenth-century preacher, read *The Pilgrim's Progress* a hundred times during his ministry and stated that Bunyan had skillfully bled Scripture straight into his great literary masterpiece. Read it and you will find it difficult to disagree with that conclusion.

Here is my most cherished extract from the book, with my favourite character 'Mr Valiant-for-Truth' as he reaches the Celestial City. Is he not someone to aspire to? As my life is shortened it is possibly too late and I acknowledge that. I am sure about my place in the next world because Jesus took the burden of my sins just as He took Christian's burden at the cross. However, I have fallen a long way behind this great spiritual giant of a character in life. Perhaps it's not too late for others though? ... Could you, with the help of God, be like 'Mr Valiant-for-Truth'?

Read this quote carefully and think about it ... enjoy and meditate on it. Above all, get a copy of the book! Being brought up using the King James version of the Bible, I cannot see past the original version, but you can download the complete book in more modern language.

'After this it was noised abroad that Mr. Valiant-for-Truth was taken with a summons, by the same post as the other; and had this for a token that the summons was true, *"That his pitcher was broken at the fountain."* When he understood it, he called for his friends, and told them of it. Then, said he, I am going to my Father's; and though with great difficulty I have got hither, yet now I do not repent me of all the trouble I have been at to arrive where I am. My sword I give to him that shall succeed me in my pilgrimage, and my courage and skill to him that can get it. My marks and scars I carry with me, to be a witness for me that I have fought His battles who will now be my rewarder. When the day that he must go hence was come, many accompanied him to the river-side, into which as he went, he said, "*Death, where is thy sting?*" And as he went down deeper, he said, "*Grave, where is thy victory?*" So he passed over, and all the trumpets sounded for him on the other side.'

Going AWOL

This story is one which, initially, I thought was too personal to share, but then I realised that it could be helpful to people. In some respects, it is a sad and painful memory, but like so many of life's bumps, there is some value, release and even amusement in revisiting that day ... shocking to think that I am going back forty-five years!

School was not my favourite place! Annoying teachers told my parents that I ought to be doing much better. This led my father to take it on himself to help me with algebra. I can count reasonably well but never could do algebra! Dad clearly thought that I was having him on, claiming not to understand basic formulas and we had a huge shouting match about it. Upset, angry and frustrated, I noisily threw down the school book and stormed out of the house, the dog following me in support. Those of you who knew my dad will be aware that he was not someone to mess around with!

I knew that my dad, as an ex-army man of his time, would undoubtedly consider my outburst to be sheer insubordination. So, on what was a dull, cold, February afternoon, I took to the hills, depressed, and feeling that I had now burned my boats. I walked for some miles over moor

Murdo and his dad

and hill, till there was that great feeling that I had escaped from it all. In a strange way, I felt a strong sense that God was present. The Bible makes it clear that God is 'omnipresent'. We can get away from people, places and problems but never from God.

It was clear to me on that grey day that God was there, all powerful and in total control. Looking back down the years I wish that I could somehow regain that strong sense of His presence, power, and ability to preserve me today.

This may seem strange from a twenty-first-century perspective, but a visiting preacher from Fort William phoned my parents about four hours prior to my return home. He didn't know me or them, but said, 'The boy is fine so do not worry.' He had been praying and had a strong sense that I was okay – a strong enough sense that he decided to phone and reassure them.

The big danger of course was hypothermia. Many people on a moderately cold, damp night in the Highland hills will get as wet as I did, and, unaware of a low body temperature, perish. I was, of course, oblivious to the fact that I was a prime candidate for that condition. Maybe my sheer angst kept me going?

To continue with the escapade, I went from Balmacara over to the Plockton area as darkness enveloped. There I calmed down a bit more and wisely started the five mile journey by single track road back to Kyle, hiding when cars passed.

What would I say to my father? How could I explain my bad temper? Would I get the dreaded belting? On coming close to Kyle, Sandy the little dog, made a dash for home and was quickly captured and taken to my parents. I hid in the bushes at the bottom of the garden as I realised that half the village was out looking for me.

Knowing every inch of the moor behind the house (now Wemyss Place), I went there and wondered if I could nip in the back door without being seen and by some miracle find an excuse for being back in the house. My pride dictated that I did not want to be found by any of my friends. North, south and east, lines of torch lights lit up the hills. Then it dawned on me that there was an enormous, well-organised, search party combing the area. How excruciatingly embarrassing! Could a hole in the ground somehow swallow me? Probably not ...

Eventually very cold and tired, I gave myself up to the mercy of the kindly local headmaster and was taken home at around midnight to the great relief of my parents. They had naturally been worried sick. To be fair to my father, he realised that he had gone over the top. After a welcome hot bath, the doctor called and saw that, despite the adventure, I was in rude health. Listening to my grovelling apology for the trouble I had caused, Dr Adamson chuckled in his very distinctive manner and said, 'Actually this has been a great thing for the health of the village: it really got people walking the streets, moors and hills!'

So, what are the lessons learned?

Firstly: if you just cannot do algebra, art or Latin, give up on it and find something you are good at.

Secondly: instead of considering my dad to be an ogre, it would have been good to recognise that he wanted the best start in life for me. However, he should have seen that, although I had some strong points, an academic career was not to be my future.

Then, of course, there are the concerned, big-hearted, Kyle residents who spent hours searching for me, fearing for my wellbeing. Whatever impression the twenty-first-century tabloids give us, my experience in life has been that the vast majority of people are so very decent.

What about God? He is still everywhere and has absolute control over the world He created. It's just hard sometimes to see and appreciate that great fact. He has certainly poured many blessings on me, that is despite the fact that I am still the same stubborn character as I was at the age of twelve.

Arson and Burglary

The polling day for the local elections on 12th May, 1970, is forever imprinted on my mind! It truly could not have started better. It was, after all, a holiday from school and a fine dry day with a westerly breeze. My parents decided to travel eighty miles to Inverness for the day. They left the children to have meals with grandparents down the road, so the family house was locked.

My friends and I took tents up the hill to a grassy area among the heather. This was great fun! Of course, in order to get a camp established, a fire was essential, so I went down to the house for matches, but the doors were locked. Being smaller, my eight-year-old brother, Ian, was put through the window. This would also help to diffuse any blame!

The camp fire was, in every sense, a roaring success; it was good to be out of sight, well away from pesky, nosy, interfering adults. Some of the younger boys took dry grass and made torches; this was simply the best fun ever. After all, what could be better than chasing each other with genuine burning torches! One boy, Ali Fraser, ran away from the grassy area, accidentally dropped his torch in the heather and set it on fire. To be fair to Ali, he did his utmost to beat it out with a stick, but it just kept growing ... and growing ... and growing. Ali even singed his hair quite badly as the inferno grew out of the dry heather. Helped by a westerly breeze, it raced across the hill at an extraordinary pace so there was only one thing to do ... scarper!

How could this misfortune be explained to my parents? Could I somehow shift the blame? After all, I had not *actually* started the fire, which by the time they arrived home at 9 pm was still raging fiercely across the Lochalsh hills. Every available fire fighter in the area was working hard to keep it away from telegraph poles and the young trees of Balmacara Estate.

I couldn't decide what was worse – meeting the firemen or the policeman? However, that all paled into insignificance compared to explaining my actions to my poor father.

My sympathetic grandparents, Alec and Bessie Prosser, promised faithfully to put a word in for me when my parents returned in the evening. In all of my twelve years I had NEVER been in so much trouble. The thought of the eight-fingered belt which had belonged to my great-great-grandfather, John Prosser, who had been a schoolmaster on Skye, did not particularly bother me. It was just knowing that I had been an absolute idiot and that I deserved what was coming ... and even a bit more!

Inevitably the police visited in their blue Ford Anglia, rightly identifying me as both the ringleader and culprit. The kid who organised the matches fairly and squarely had to take most of the blame!

The eight-fingered belt was used but, to this day, the sheer embarrassment and shame I felt was a far greater punishment.

In my years of flying round Scotland I have been privileged to see many a billowing, raging, spectacular heather fire from the air; of course the vast majority are on grouse moors and are good for general wildlife.

Our fire burned for two days so at one level a great job was done! They do say that it is an ill wind that blows nobody any good! Am I just making excuses again?

Looking back to childhood more than forty-five years on, I still cringe thinking about my sheer stupidity. Thank goodness nobody was hurt or even killed.

I take great comfort from the prayer of David in Psalm 25 verse 7: *'Remember not the sins of my youth, nor my transgressions.'*

The amazing Kyle Firefighters

An Excellent Teacher

Many of my teacher friends and relatives are understandably disappointed to learn that I gained very little from school, which seemed to me like something akin to prison, or at least cruelty to children, for seven hours a day. However it is true, spiritually as well as in the secular world, that unpleasant and even 'wilderness experiences' can strengthen us and make us adaptable, resilient and practical.

In 1963 I was dragged to school both kicking and screaming on my first day. Life had been very fulfilling but perhaps a bit unregimented up to that point. My teacher, Miss Cameron, had been one of the 1930s evacuees from the remote Atlantic island of St Kilda, no doubt a good enough teacher, but this young man was determined not to co-operate in any way whatsoever.

I have four distinct memories of the three years in her care.

Firstly: Dyslexia was not acknowledged till decades later so I was the complete dunce with a fully paid seat in the bad corner, a hopeless basket or remedial case!

Secondly: To my young mind at least, dotting out the shape of a donkey with a blunt pin seemed like a pointless exercise. So instead I placed the stupid thing on the desk and quickly traced round it with the pin, rather than make individual piercings. I was finished in two minutes flat having, as a by-product, etched a very fine looking donkey on to a Highland Council desk. A huge telling off followed, but I well remember boasting that at least I had produced a far superior result to my friends!

Thirdly: The daily pre-lunch treat was to create models with plasticine, and the expectation from day to day was to maintain the various vivid colours as long as possible. No nice, wee, matchstick men or happy, colourful, families for me: plasticine was instead rolled up into a mottled, then grey, ball and monsters, war machines and horrible scary hybrids were spawned!

Fourthly: It took all of twenty-five minutes to amble the 600 yards to school and still be intentionally late. However, it was only three to four minutes from a sitting start to sprint 300 yards across heather and bog home to the back door, the nanosecond the bell rang.

At the tender age of eight, following three years of wilderness experience, my life was just about to open out into valuable, interesting, and productive years of education ... possibly the only two years of formal engaged education I would ever derive benefit from.

Miss Cameron saw no point in my advancing to the next class, but the Primary 4 and 5 teacher, Miss Stewart, took me on as a project, and the next two years revealed that she must have utilised the correct psychology.

'MURDO!' she would declare, 'You know how they cut the rust out of cars at your dad's garage?' 'Yes,' I said ... where on earth is this going? I thought. 'Well, I am going to cut the rust out of your brain, so you had better work hard for me!' Imagine giving such a blunt wake-up call to a pupil today!

Before too long, with some parental help, my homework was consistent, correct, and applauded. Recognising a glimmer of dramatic ability I was soon reading with passion and expression to the class having been given a weekly slot.

Miss Stewart was clearly one to push boundaries and was absolutely right to rehabilitate my three Rs, but her cringe-worthy step too far was to have me sing Psalm 23 to the class.

'Get it out of the boots!' 'Project your voice.' 'More expression.' 'Get the great meaning into it.'

'THE LORD IS MY SHEPHERD. HE RESTORES MY SOUL ... You would not think that listening to you! I WILL DWELL IN THE HOUSE OF THE LORD FOREVER? Make it credible boy!'

Years later, going round local churches preaching, I always insisted on taking a precentor for the singing, having realised that music was not a natural talent of mine. Sometimes, I would take my young brother, Ian, who has a good voice and can hold a tune. Hymns and psalms badly sung can sound awful. Simon Cowell, you never met my teacher, but she could teach you a technique or two!

Can you imagine the reaction of my friends? Absolute dunce to teacher's pet in just a term! In order to prove that I was still one of the guys, I pushed a boy off a rock we called 'the high jump' into soft, dirty, peaty ground. He was well messed up, so my classmates arrested me, and frog-marched me to Miss Stewart. The predictable punishment was a belting; for a slender woman she could inflict pain just as well as any strapping man. Of course, I totally deserved and accepted this just and fair punishment.

Miss Charlotte Stewart had high expectations from her special project but she was to be disappointed. After leaving her classroom, the rust she had cut away through her encouragement and high hopes came back, and for the rest of my time in school, I just blended in, keeping my head below the parapet, producing mediocre results. Years later I bumped into her and reading between the lines (not the ones she often gave as punishment), it was clear that her expectation had been high. However, she very graciously wished me well in my chosen career path.

What a difference a good teacher and some encouragement can make!

Ouch!

These days there is rightly much talk about stamping out bullying. Intimidation and physical attacks by older boys were part of life as a first-year pupil at Plockton School. A good kicking from the older boys was just a rite of passage. However, I was kicked in an unfortunate place. BOY DID IT HURT! After an embarrassing examination by the GP, my parents had to explain to me that there was a risk that I would never be able to father children without an operation!

At age twelve, parenting seemed to be a distant concept. Fear of the fairly simple operation and the prospect of a week eighty miles away was daunting, although I knew it was important. In

Spring 1971, I arrived at the RNI (Royal Northern Infirmary) in Inverness for the operation.

The fifteen or so other patients in my ward varied in age from sixteen to mid-seventies and I was very quickly included in the rapport and banter. There were a couple of very ill patients who did not have much to say. This deeply moved me and taught me that our health is more important than our bank balance. The great spiritual question of what happens when we breathe our last, was also something to face up to at that time.

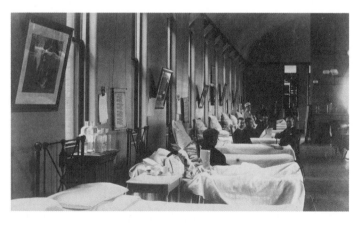

Typical hospital ward of the time

There was an American man unashamedly over to enjoy a free hernia operation courtesy of the NHS. Nice fellow that he was, I rightly considered him to be a bit of a user. A burly, jovial, Inverness butcher was in the bed next to me. He seemed to know everybody and was a friend to all. His outrageous flirting with the nurses was highly entertaining. Nigel, a sixteen-year-old boy took me under his wing as we exchanged books and comics.

One of my new friends decided that we should all bet on a horse at twenty pence a go. I won £3 and knowing that my father, with his black and white reasoning, would totally disapprove, I discretely off-loaded the money to one of the old men. Had I kept it, the operation could have been the least of my worries. My father would feel he had failed miserably, if he knew his son had subscribed to any form of gambling. I've always taken the view that there are worse evils to correct in the world before tackling that one! However, those of you who take my father's view will be pleased to know that I have never wagered since that day.

The experience in hospital, though un-pleasant in many ways, taught me a lot about life and although such bullying has been curbed in the twenty-first century the psychological bullying experienced by youngsters, seems to me to be harder to deal with. Without diminishing the seriousness of this issue, at least my experience was honest straightforward bullying! If indeed there is such a thing?

As much as the good experiences, bumps, scrapes and hard questions of life mould us into the people we become; would I be a slightly different person today had I not been hospitalised? Probably, though it's hard to tell. God, however, knows.

I sense that you have a slightly awkward question … *Was the operation successful?* I have three great grown-up children!

Revival!

In the twenty-first century church, there is a reluctance to talk of deep spiritual experience as well as anything regarding the supernatural.

Secular Scotland, in past centuries 'The Land of the Book', is now about as far away as you could get from a God-fearing nation. In my experience, there is tacit agreement that spiritual matters are not discussed. No doubt some people are even ashamed of their gullible, Bible-believing forebears.

There have been great times of spiritual awakening since the Reformation. The Free Church, which I belong to, was indeed born out of great revival in 1843! These days are long gone and such zeal across Scotland seems very remote now.

Back in 1970, God worked among the young people of my hometown, Kyle of Lochalsh. I have never experienced anything like it since that time of extraordinary blessing, forty-five years ago. Around fifteen young people came to faith.

Any book worth reading on the subject of Christian revival will major on the fact that people pleaded constantly with God in earnest prayer for months, years and even decades before God worked in a powerful manner. Kyle was no exception. For years, believers had prayed for young lives to be changed. Their prayers were answered when two young men from the Faith Mission came and held meetings. They were very inexperienced (perhaps even wet behind the ears!), yet God worked through them in a powerful manner. The majority of those who came to faith were changed in such a way that it could truly be compared to darkness and light; the whole community had to take stock of what had happened.

Just as the great Kilsyth revival in the 1750s rippled out to Gargunnock, near Stirling, where I now live, it pleased God in the early 70s to work in places like Kyleakin across the water from Kyle and Glenelg down the coast.

The local Kyle Primary School had committed Christians as teachers and they made sure that the Bible was taught to a very high standard. The Psalms were learned by heart in Sunday school and although I found church very dreary and – to be frank – plain boring, the great truths expressed in the Bible had an impact on me and I accepted it as the inspired Word of God at a young age. I started attending a meeting held in the Scout Hut on a Sunday evening. This meeting had started as a result of so many young people coming to faith.

The tin hut was musty with cobwebs, and had cracked brown linoleum and creaky wooden benches. It had been a gift to the village from the Americans who had taken it to Kyle at the time of World War I. Miraculously it still stands today! On attending the first meeting, I recognised immediately that there was something different. There was such enthusiasm for the new-found faith, a real thirst to learn more, a desire to praise God. Some voices may not have hit the note, the old piano was out of tune and had a few dead keys, yet a joyful noise was made, the roof was just about raised on many occasions!

What made this different? I firmly believe that God the Holy Spirit was at work in a special manner. It was a bit like the contrast between a low pixel black and white image and high resolution 3D colour. There was such liberty in prayer, such joy, peace, awe and hope. There was no doubt that the Holy Spirit was there! These people, some of them just a couple of years older than myself, had been TRANSFORMED, given a new heart and a desire to follow God.

In High School, a very sceptical attitude prevailed strongly among many pupils and some of the teachers, '*Religion has made people mad!*' On one occasion a brave, recently converted fifteen-year-old boy preached a sermon in the cloakroom at lunchtime. The wonderful subject for a mainly hostile audience was 'Heaven'. One detractor got up and, without even questioning the existence of both heaven and hell, gave a counter talk on what a great place hell would be as his friends would be with him. Both protagonist and antagonist have gone to their eternal reward. As they say, life is short.

Trying to counter the strong influences affecting me, my biology teacher, an exceptionally nice man, made it very clear that the Bible, in his opinion, was a fairy story. The chemistry teacher went further; in front of the class he jokingly presented a picture of me in my loft on a Sabbath afternoon studying the catechism, when based on my exam results, studying chemistry would be more appropriate. Of course, I knew of a dimension these well-meaning men knew nothing of; they had not experienced the power and presence of God the Holy Spirit at work. In these days, it was said from time to time that in twenty years and certainly by the millennium there would be no Free Church. How misguided: God had other ideas, as today we see green shoots of recovery within and beyond the denomination. Worldwide expansion of the gospel is another great encouragement to believers.

Sadly, as seems to be the case in other accounts of revival, some turn back after a period of time and that was the case in Kyle. However, the majority, who by the grace of God persevered, went on to influence many others toward the Kingdom of God. Eternity alone will reveal the total impact of that albeit small revival. Over the years, I have attended some churches where there has been great emphasis on the person and work of God the Holy Spirit but never has anything come EVEN CLOSE to my experience as we shared fellowship in that old hut.

Fast forward forty-five years and with the psalmist David, I *'call to mind the days of old,'* and think on these marvellous times of blessing. God has never allowed me to experience anything like it since. Of course, it is refreshing to know of people here and there coming to faith, but that deep intensity does not appear to be obvious in the church of today. God has showered me with so many material blessings in this life, I WOULD GLADLY FORFEIT ALL OF THEM if only I could once again see His mighty hand at work and hear of a massive awakening in Scotland, as now, terminally ill, I live out my final few months on earth.

The Ongoing Fight for Life

The instinct within the vast majority of us is to live, and indeed live useful, productive, satisfying lives. My bad diagnosis highlighted the horror of a shattered and now very different, fading life. Friends, family, and even acquaintances have been so good. My wife, Margaret, has been a rock. With me no longer able to perform some very basic tasks, she is lovingly dedicated to making life easier in the time left.

The big dilemma of 14th November, 2016, was to choose one of the following three options:

- Surgery to remove a tissue sample for analysis leading to the correct radio or chemotherapy?
- Do nothing and fade away over the next three months?

- Remove as much as possible of the tumour requiring a frightening operation called an 'Awake craniotomy'?

The third option, which I chose, radical as it sounded, could only give nine months to a year of quality life, if successful. Every instinct within me, despite strong confidence in the afterlife, cried out that it was right to put my life in the hands of the surgeon, Imran Liaquat, and his excellent team. I am amazed and humbled

Murdo and Margaret

that they were willing to put dedicated staff as well as costly effort into extending the life of a terminally ill, fifty-eight-year-old, optimist. The operation lasted six hours. Bone removal was under general anaesthetic. They then woke me up for four hours of delicate tumour removal with my head firmly clamped. The trick was to keep me talking. Margaret assured the anaesthetist that I could talk for Britain and maybe even Europe! Hopefully the dialogue was not too boring for them. From time to time the surgeon was able to check that my arm and leg movement remained intact.

What about permanent healing direct from God? I still pray for that and am calmed by the fact that a worldwide army of people are indeed praying! Social media and blogging truly has global reach. We live in AMAZING times!

Prayer was felt and appreciated on that day. As I used to remind Margaret when flying light aircraft to the Highlands and Islands, 'I will leave this scene of time only when God dictates!'

Beyond Courage and Awake Brain Surgery

At one time I had responsibility for a Lancia dealer who was extremely proud of his family motto '*Courage*' set in stone at the entrance to his hereditary castle. My Clan motto is '*With undaunted heart*'. Sadly, both these virtues, despite my best efforts, have had a habit of eluding me.

But what about courage facing a brutal emergency brain operation? There was no courage needed simply because I looked to the One who conquered death itself. Do not think that I have not struggled spiritually or doubted, but I went through that operation at peace and with strong faith in the Word of God ... May these words from the end of Romans 8 someday give you the comfort which they gave me over the past few days ...

> For I am sure that neither death nor life, nor angels nor rulers, nor things present nor things to come, nor powers, nor height nor depth, nor anything else in all creation, will be able to separate us from the love of God in Christ Jesus our Lord.
>
> (Romans 8:38-39 ESV)

I felt calmness when going to the Western General in Edinburgh on Monday, 5th December. This is where faith felt and expressed for a lifetime was being tested. I had an unwavering conviction that here, by the river of death, God was comforting me and giving me assurance. Some of my thoughts the previous week, frankly, had been quite dark.

Following full preparation, my confidence in Mr Liaquat, Dr Midgely and the team of twelve was absolute. They all demonstrated a high degree of both professionalism and concern and I could sense that they were pleased to have a willing, confident, calm patient for the six-hour, relatively uncommon, procedure.

As they prepared to put me completely under anaesthetic for the two-hour scalp opening to the motor strip of the brain, where there was by now a ragged, very nasty looking aggressive cancerous tumour, apologies were made for the lack of organisation within the larger than expected theatre full of monitors and equipment. This was them disorganised? All this just to give me a year of extra life in the lower world?

Out I went like a light without feeling a thing, to wake in a bit of a dream, conscious of people working hard to make me comfortable. When told to move an arm I gratefully obeyed. I was warned that there could be pain where my scalp was clamped in four places, but NOT one spasm was felt. The four hours quickly passed in a dopey but adequately functional state. They kept me awake, expertly applying local anaesthetic, while stapling my head back together. On reaching the recovery room with tubes all over my body and high on morphine, I was told that the operation had been a great success: 80 percent of the tumour would have been a victory, 90 percent was a truly outstanding result.

Later that day, both Mr Liaquat and Dr Midgely visited me in the High Dependency Ward. I felt so grateful for their skill, having come right through without even a hint of pain.

I wish I could report that all the patients in the High Dependency Unit were progressing and comfortable, but sadly over the next few days, I was to witness both raw and frightening suffering. One woman waiting for a similar operation had haemorrhaged and just wanted to die. My heart and prayers went out to both her and her distraught, supportive family.

An Edinburgh man, who had a lifetime of experience in the Royal Mile tourist trade, had a badly infected wound, despite his tumour operation being straightforward. Intravenous morphine drips and various nasty procedures kept him alive as pain came and went. On every occasion, he had just the right words of encouragement for each of us in the room. A truly remarkable as well as stoic character!

A young man, thirty years my junior, was constantly vomiting or in pain following his tumour resection and I felt quite pessimistic regarding his future. Brain tumours, even today, take healthy people of any age.

A recently retired headmaster had just undergone the first part of an arduous procedure to protect his spinal cord. He still needs months of hospital treatment to be cured. Again, the pain was very obvious. Thankfully his care was the very best and most cheerful.

For me, to be released after five days with no complications makes me so thankful. They say on the internet to always remember that the letters MD stand for 'medical doctorate' and not *'medical deity'*. On catching a flashing glimpse of my surgeon, Imran Liaquat, in the side mirror of the car as we drove away, my instantaneous personal reflection was that he does not consider himself to be a *'medical deity'* any more than I think that *'brain surgeon'* could have been my calling in life!

In the meantime, I am not quite ready to ask God that great car journey question, ARE WE THERE YET? But I would still like to do a bit of damage ... if He allows me. Given my ongoing cheek towards her, the robust mother-in-law has contributed the opinion that it could be a while yet!

Into the Light

Since my youth, flying light aircraft has been a great hobby. The varied challenges and distances I chose to travel, mainly in the glorious Highlands and Islands, meant that it fitted me like a glove. My Uncle Murdo had been a World War II pilot and going up with him in his plane gave me a yearning for the freedom of the skies, so I trained as a private pilot in the mid-eighties.

I flew for thirty years, covering around 600 hours at the controls. Experience was beginning to make up for lack of week to week practice by the day of my final pre-brain tumour flight with my youngest son, Duncan. We flew from Stornoway to Glasgow in bad weather on 28th July, 2016.

If there was ever any excuse to travel by air I would always volunteer. A combination of the freedom, the skill and the perspective of that amazing dimension had me hooked. When weather was poor (so often the case in Scotland), the burning question asked at Cumbernauld would be, 'Is it flyable?' and Ian Haggis the CFI (Chief Flying Instructor) would then ask a further question, 'Is it Murdo-able?' The trick was to thoroughly understand both Highland weather limits and cross wind limits and he gave me much in the way of sensible, realistic advice over the years.

Murdo about to fly

Going back to the late nineties, I was not as experienced in mountain flying. My mother was hospitalised in Inverness so I visited, then took the short flight in worsening weather across to visit my father in Kyle via a very remote long narrow loch called Mullardoch which runs East to West above Glen Affric. The cloud seemed to come right down as I battled a stiff headwind and was buffeted ten miles along that uninhabited, deserted stretch of water with dark foreboding cliffs on each side. Unable to risk turning because of the narrow space and knowing that inevitably if I flew into cloud I would hit a hillside, fear took hold of me. Yet, the instruments all read green, the artificial horizon said the plane was straight and level, the loch surface was still well below me. To my shame TERROR began to grip me; if I ended up having to ditch, would my body ever be found? Would another great Highland air mystery be created?

I now make an inevitable spiritual comparison, as I am finding myself in a valley looking forward some months to what is, to my mind, premature death. I make the same assertion as David in Psalm 23: *'You are with me.'* Is God really there I hear you ask with a bit of doubt in your voice. ABSOLUTELY is my answer. An ancient book packed with simple promises tells me of the God of love in Christ who conquered death itself, who is risen and even now beckoning me to that bright and better land.

To put it bluntly, I am either just a pile of decaying matter going nowhere or a great creature created in the image of God; the latter is my firm belief and there is no room whatsoever for middle ground or a neutral position.

Meanwhile, back in the cockpit the gauges are still green and through my headphones a quiet, clear, loving and reassuring voice says ... *'Fear not for I am with you.'*

All these years ago I physically came into bright sunlight at the end of the valley that day and managed to very quickly laugh off the doubts and fears of the journey. Expecting a real greaser of a landing the day my Saviour takes me home to glory ... in the meantime, I invite you to consider the claims of Jesus ... Or are you going to insist that you are just a pile of lousy chemicals?

The Boss

On completion of my degree in being a 'Garage Man' and then a much acclaimed PhD in 'How to Modify Rusty 1950s Car Parts to fit 1970s Cars' as well as 'The Negative Effects of Wester Ross Vehicle Corrosion' it was now time for a new career challenge which was to last for seven years … the perfect number.

On moving to Inverness in March 1982 my new boss, Donald Mackenzie, had an impressive Fiat garage and showroom in the busy Tomnahurich Street which led to the Ness Bridge and into the High Street. I remember well the happiness, comfort and ease of working with him.

My previous place of learning had been very casual. The dress code was a scruffy boiler suit, the more threadbare and dirty the better! I thought that my nice worn brown leather jacket would be good for the new job but was quickly told to wear my suit. My only suit was a green, striped, flared, three-piece effort from the late 70s. Stylish! A fortunate travelling salesman had sold me the top quality material which no other idiot wanted and I'd proudly had the alarming outfit made to measure! The good people of Inverness must have had a laugh. Just to top it off, for some reason I wore it with a brown mottled tie.

Murdo with Donald Mackenzie 'The Boss'

The boss, who very quickly baptized me Murd, would, even from across the town, sense when a car sale had been made. Other times he would enquire 150 feet along the showroom ... 'Murd!' A slow response and it would be 'MURD!' then 'MURDO'. 'Did you sell that car? When will it go out?' Some of my friends became very good at mimicking and even embellishing some of the conversation.

At that time, my role within the church was to go around the Highlands taking services. Rev M.A. Macleod was then the minister of the local Greyfriars Free Church and 'The Boss' regularly skipped his own church to hear a really good communicator. Cassette tapes of the sermons which he passed to me were thought-provoking and much discussion and analysis followed. He would often ask my opinion on a finer point of doctrine and if I had not listened properly (or at all) he would know perfectly well as he watched me flounder. Looking back, I can now see how he quietly and very cleverly tutored me.

'Come here, Murd,' Donald called one day. 'It's bad news. Fiat are making us send you on a course. Do not worry about the pedantic speaker up the front, talk to the wee man next to you and you will learn a lot.' Thirty-five years on, having had my fill of courses, seminars, conventions, assemblies, presbyteries etc., my advice to any of you willing to listen, is the same as that of the Boss ... listen to that wee man next to you and gain real insight!

What about his own unique selling techniques which had contributed so much to his success in life? HE WAS THE MASTER. Consider this scene, the young man, me, was not quite closing the sale so he would invite both the customer and myself to his office. With a big grin and tongue firmly in cheek he would open his jacket, show our victim the torn inside lining and talk of the need for a new suit. The worn brogues came in handy as well. The deal was right now sealed amid much hilarity.

Lillah, was a very efficient accountant and is also owed a debt for some of the lessons learned. I would drone on about all my great youth work in the church. One day she cracked up and said, 'You idiot! One would think that the church consists of only young people listening to nonsense from fools like yourself.'

As Proverbs says, 'Faithful are the wounds of a friend.' Salesmen by nature are a complex temperamental breed and there can be a need from time to time to expertly deflate stratospheric egos. She had the buttons at her fingertips and knew exactly when to press them! 'The Boss', on the other hand, had the same little keyboard in his pocket but used the buttons a bit more subtly.

Lillah retired to her native Orkney a few years later and my shockingly easy-going work environment which, over the years, had allowed me to come and go to work as I pleased, gave me the freedom to fly up one nice day to visit her in her new home. I remember laughing for hours with her and her husband about all the past pantomimes of Tomnahurich Street. On my return I didn't touch down in Dalcross Airport till after dusk. I received a real dressing down from the Chief Instructor for my lack of contact, lack of professionalism and pathetic timekeeping! Today, in a society obsessed with structures and regulations, even flying to the little airfields of Coastal and Island Scotland you usually need permission, authority in triplicate and extra insurance.

The eighties were in so many ways great days of freedom and twenty-first century folk including myself, sadly are so uptight and driven by materialism and status. I wish we could return to the easy-going nature of the business in Tomnahurich Street created by 'The Boss' where a young and middle-aged man both considered talking about eternal issues to be more life-enhancing than reaching sales targets. We even sometimes simply took the time to just watch the world go by. For your information, most of the sales targets were still exceeded. But I don't think it would have mattered that much supposing we had fallen slightly short!

The Murchison family circa 1995

In His Hands

This is being written on a dull mid-December day. To be perfectly frank with you, I am a long way removed from that great assurance of Psalm 91: 'With long life will I satisfy him' or the blessing to the servant of God in Psalm 128:6 (NIV): *'May you live to see your children's children.'*

Growing up witnessing the long, productive lives of my forebears it was always observed and indeed acknowledged that God had given me an excellent set of genes. Was ninety years possible? Or in the brave new world of twenty-first century medical science, would it be cheeky to look forward to 100 years of life?

Hopes, dreams, illusions, and even common sense plans were totally shattered on the 30th of August when I took a massive seizure, so bad that the family thought I had died. Life is now defined and talked of in terms of my pre- and post-seizure lifestyle. Following the seizure I was diagnosed with a low grade brain tumour. Eight weeks later, following further scans, the tumour had leap-frogged to being a grade 4, aggressive, cancerous one and I was given three months to live.

Desire to remain active had previously been very strong and I was always thankful to God that both resilience and a good level of fitness had stayed with me over the decades. Born in 1958, I looked ahead just a couple of years to sixty years of blessed and varied life. Fast forward again into my sixties and who knows what great business deals I could have done. Having been blessed materially, a number of exciting future adventures could even be planned.

Then there was church work. Having been involved with setting up a new church in Stirling, even more skills could have been developed and others could have been motivated. So, the burning question has to be, 'Why God? Why cut this off? Seriously, and with submissive respect, GOD WHY?'

The psalmist prays, '*My God in mid time of my days take thou me not away.*' (Psalm 102:24)[1] reminds me I am not the only one struggling. People of faith down the millennia have questioned the providence, and indeed the will of God, for them. When peace of mind goes we struggle, and it is then that the words of David resonate, '*Amid the multitude of thoughts which in my heart do fight my soul lest it be overcharg'd thy comforts do delight*' (Psalm 94:19)[2].

The surgeon, Imran Liaquat, thanked me for willingly allowing him to push boundaries with risk of losing motor movement in an uncommon operation called an 'awake craniotomy'. Of course, I am the one indebted to him as there was not much to lose, knowing that the tumour had both doubled and changed course in just six weeks. Mr Liaquat reckons that with the correct combination of chemo and radiotherapy, a year of reasonable quality life may be possible. God, of course, knows. As the psalmist said, '*My times are in thy hand*' (Psalm 31:15). I will not depart one second before His summons.

1. www.psalm-singing.org/psalms/scottish-1650
2. www.psalm-singing.org/psalms/scottish-1650

So, is there any hope of a cure? YES, the God I trust could, in an instant, cure me. He is sovereign; His control is absolute; He is bringing human history to a climax and my life has played only a very tiny part. Yes, I do want to be cured and, having enjoyed working in the vineyard, remain there for a while yet. In the fourteen weeks of this new journey, a remarkable number of people have told me stories of miraculous total healings which defy cutting edge medicine and, even though my natural tendency is to sceptism, I believe most of them ... please keep praying.

In the meantime, what can I do to promote the great news of salvation? Mid-September, a little bit bored but previously having been a total mocker of social media, daughter Sarah set me up on Facebook and I started posting photos and experiences. When you have the glorious gospel to share, a Facebook page is simply not enough so, I graduated to blogging and 1,000 people a day have been following my posts from as far and wide as Azerbaijan, Australia, Canada, Mexico and Europe (to name a few). I was never even remotely interested in writing articles pre-seizure, but He has given me an unexpected but seemingly effective new ministry. Supposing you had told me as recently as this past summer that I would be Facebooking and blogging by autumn then, believe me, I would have LOL'd (similarly, if you'd told me I'd be using the acronym LOL, I would have laughed out loud at you!).

What about that impending day of departure then? Leaving earthly goods behind, making wills, changing business directors, selling stuff and the responsible passing down of assets has been a nightmare as well as a huge emotional roller-coaster. My advice to you is, while keeping the comparative limited value of material blessings in perspective, sort out your earthly affairs now and give you dear family less stress should a crisis occur. My family have been great and I could not have wished for better. The business is now leased out and, for now, trades under the previous name.

Both Margaret and the children have rallied round and given me the very best of help and comfort in terms of this world. There is, however, the thought of departure and that strong conviction that the place of many mansions beckons. We think of heaven as a shadow-land far more real than this lower world. I always remember C.S. Lewis in one of his books, *The Great Divorce*, talking of the grass of heaven cutting the feet of new arrivals.

No fear then? Well, certainly there was no fear on the 5th of December when I had the surgery: God gave sufficient strength. However, I have to confess that with a degree of recovery, some trepidation reappears. What if all I have is a crutch or placebo effect? The foil to such gloomy thoughts is the logic of an inspired, God-breathed book and a Saviour who went through the horror of death to make it painless for me. That great statement in *The Shorter Catechism*, 'The souls of believers are at their death made perfect in holiness and pass immediately into glory', resonates now in an extremely powerful manner.

However close your dear family are, you go to the grave without them, but you do have a friend, who sticks closer than any brother – Jesus Christ, the righteous one.

See you on the other side, then, in a world where the last enemy will have been conquered ... FOREVER.

Enforced Retirement

When is the right time to retire? For me, sixty would have been good, with plans to travel, projects to undertake, church work and a large garden awaiting my attention. Don't tell Margaret, but maybe I would have bought an old light aircraft and gone on an age-defying adventure! We can of course dream and plan all we like, but in the final analysis each breath we take depends on the will of God whether we like it or not. Now, terminally ill, with a brain tumour at the tender age of fifty-eight, I have to accept that my working life is over as I hop one step along in front of the funeral director.

Enough gloom and doom! Despite headwinds, it has been tremendously satisfying over the past twenty-five years, against all the odds, to build the business from virtually nothing to a fairly successful garage, as well as a property-leasing business.

Despite a few gripes, the motor trade has really been very good to me and I am the third generation of my family to be in it. My younger brother, Ian, has an even more remarkable claim, being the third generation in the Kyle of Lochalsh business, M. Murchison & Sons, renamed by him to Murchison's. Not all that many small garages in Scotland have passed down through three generations!

What advice would I give to those wanting to start a business? If you have a bit of go in you, why work for someone else? On the other hand, if there is not a good deal of fire, stubbornness and tenacity in your belly, then please stay in that comfortable job. Can you live with your own mistakes? I certainly can and can testify that experience teaches fools.

My motor trade business never amounted to more than 500-600 car sales a year; the original growth came from staunch customers from the length and breadth of Scotland. Most of you were extremely loyal and I will really miss doing business with you, and I have to say that local Stirling people were also very supportive. More recently, we engaged in digital marketing which proved very successful. People would beat a track from as far as London, Shetland and even Ireland to do business.

Being your own boss is a privilege which, within reason, allows you to do as you please and, over the years, this had the distinct advantage of giving me the opportunity to engage in other activities: preaching, Gideons, local Haldane Trust, local Rotary, flying, keeping a big garden as well as general trustee work for the Free Church of Scotland. I also did a bit of property development which was very satisfying. It was a privilege to be in a position to lend out cars to missionaries home on furlough. The most recent assignment, away from business, was to spearhead a new Free Church in Stirling. This has prospered and is moving forward under the excellent leadership of Iain MacAskill as well as four elders and a deacon. Believe me when I say that, without the undoubted, as well as specific, guidance from on high it would not have succeeded. Looking back I can very clearly see the hand of God in that particular project.

Nothing, of course, stays the same. Take the Murchison Park site in Doune; it has had a few generations of owners and uses … little wonder the hymn writer penned these words, 'Change and decay in all around I see.' My life has given way and yes, I am sorry to leave the business behind, but like the hymn writer I can say this, 'On Christ the solid rock I stand.' The business in its various forms has been great. Serving the church has been rewarding. However, the real deal is that Jesus Christ has conquered death. He ultimately brings those who trust Him to heaven itself.

My family have been so very supportive and without Margaret much of what was achieved in life would not have been possible. However, there is that impending, tearful, emotional, separation, the sobering reality that just as we took nothing into this world we will take nothing out. Jesus Christ, that ignored figure in the secular Scotland of 2017, promises us a city of great beauty, of many mansions and has prepared a place for me and all who look to Him … I place my complete trust in Him.

What about yourself? Do you have hope beyond this scene of time?

A Break in the Cloud

The tumour of mid-November doubled in size and between then and my operation on 5th December, shockingly serious deterioration set in. My family, for the second time in under three months, were not holding out very much hope for me. The operation, however, was an amazing success; not ONE twinge of pain! Extremely fast healing had me at home in just four days. The care was simply superb and I have great admiration for the sheer dedication of all the professionals. In the short hospital stay they queued up to impart their very relevant wisdom in a cheerful manner. Being the type of person I am, the burning question was:

'How long do I have then? Two years?'

'No.'

'Eighteen months?'

'Unlikely.'

'Twelve months?'

'At best. But deterioration may set in faster.'

I thank them for their frankness.

Given the fact that my tumour is a 'non methylated glioblastoma multiforme' made me eligible for an international trial. The biopsy result came back from Belgium saying that the tumour has the correct receptors for a new drug administered by infusion alongside chemo and radiotherapy.

If the care was, as I said previously, superb, being on the trial programme has powered it beyond superb! An extra scan now shows a tumour the size of a pea and a slightly smaller fragment. Considerable expenses to and from the hospital for six weeks are generously covered, more checks than I can recount have been carried out along with continual assurances that, apart from my brain, I am in a good state of health. Every precaution seems to have been both covered and explained in terms of side effects.

Of course, I am still terminally ill and, reading between the lines, life could now be extended by just six months. Perhaps not much, but six months extra seems good to me. People were previously taken aback when I told them that I could perhaps do a bit of damage if my Maker allows me a year. If He gives me eighteen months even more damage can be done! If He cures me and gives me a normal life span then who knows what He may want me to do as I listen to Him? ... Ears are hopefully better tuned in than previously.

Friends, both old and new, please keep praying for me; it is valued, appreciated and, believe me when I say, I can feel the effect of your pleading for me. Yes, I have my eyes set firmly on that place of many mansions, but at the same time, I do still have a strong desire to live.

Radiotherapy, oral chemotherapy and chemo by infusion will start soon. Of course, it will be difficult but if I have that peace within, which I put down to your prayers, it will be easy!

End of Trial

The cancer unit at the Western General in Edinburgh is in a pretty mundane part of the city; full marks to the architect who designed the waiting area to have spectacular views of the magnificent city and castle, which is second only to Stirling within the U.K.! The poor designer probably had to argue with unimaginative, faceless, NHS accountants to put in the large plate glass windows!

At this venue, along with radiotherapy treatment the brain tumour research team administered a dose of the possibly life-extending trial drug through an infusion. However, my temperature shot up and I was admitted to Forth Valley Hospital despite my protestations that I was fine. Following a number of blood tests, I was transferred to the Western General in Edinburgh as my liver function tests showed a dramatic increase in one of the enzymes – from 50 to 897! It turns out that I had an 'extreme adverse reaction' to either the trial drug or the chemotherapy. Fortunately, no lasting damage has been done, but it means that for me, anyway, the trial programme has come to a sudden end and I cannot have any chemotherapy for the meantime. Hopefully my bad experience will help the research team to modify this new drug which has already proved to be of value in some cases.

I was yet again looked after very well in hospital as the crisis lessened day by day, although it will be some weeks before I am back to normal. This whole trial programme, which has such complexity, reminds me of the greatest of architects – our Creator God. He made each one of us uniquely with different characteristics. Mine are proving to be a challenge for the trial drug! Joking apart, to be on the programme in the first place, my health had to be good and there was just a 33 percent chance that the tumour had the correct receptors for the drug.

With human intervention losing steam, it is now down to a powerful and sovereign God.

My confidence in Him is total and the words of Psalm 139:13-15 (ESV) speak to me powerfully:

> For you formed my inward parts; you knitted me together in my mother's womb. I praise you, for I am fearfully and wonderfully made. Wonderful are your works; my soul knows it very well. My frame was not hidden from you, when I was being made in secret, intricately woven in the depths of the earth.

So, the trial drug is not going to extend my life after all. At the end of the day, only my Creator can, if He sees fit, cure me and His Word assures me that, whilst the best and cleverest of international research programmes know a lot and are innovative and efficient, He as my Maker overrules.

Friends keep praying ... Take the time to read the whole of Psalm 139 written 3,000 years ago yet fresh, challenging, relevant and for the most part comforting, especially when considered in the light of Jesus.

It Stands Most Beautiful

Where are your roots? Mine are in what was, many years ago, a bustling village, Kyle of Lochalsh in the Highlands. As a boy I could see absolutely no reason to live anywhere else. The biggest export, however, from the Highlands is people and I was destined to leave that place at the tender age of twenty-three.

In the spring of 1989 we were living in Inverness and I had started working for Lancia, so a move to the Central Belt of Scotland was inevitable. A good relocation package was on the table with a very flexible interpretation of the term 'soft furnishings' (the excellent offer would even please a greedy politician!). The problem for us was that both the great cities of Edinburgh and Glasgow, despite the huge number of terrific houses on the market, did not somehow appeal. Both Margaret and myself are from the country. Normally quite decisive, we simply could not make up our minds. The pleasant market town of Stirling appealed, but we somehow could not find the right four-bedroom property.

I first drove through Gargunnock in April 1989, the fine new houses at the Glebe were being built and at £100,000 the one we aspired to was just slightly too ambitious. In new Drummond Place there was a split level house for £93,000, and being allowed some expenses paid trips, Margaret joined me. We viewed and put in an offer, both of us just loving the village.

They say of Jerusalem, that it is the 'joy of all the earth' and that 'it stands most beautiful'. Well, Gargunnock has to be the Scottish version! We love it anyway, (without taking anything away from Jerusalem). The view is enlivened and dominated by the Highland line to the North and the extremely fertile Carse farm land. The meandering, shining River Forth and the hills behind make it a truly splendid place. There are, of course, some other very nice villages in the area but none quite like Gargunnock! The locals were (and are) very friendly, although the pathetic looking stuffed fox in the ancient pub did not look terribly appealing on our first visit. It was only when we told people that we were hoping to buy a house that lunchtime sandwiches miraculously appeared.

Iconic as it is, Ben Lomond's best angle has to be from Gargunnock. Ben Ledi is simply spectacular and Ben Vorlich, even closer, takes a bit of beating. The Bible talks of the permanence of mountains, reminding us of God's continuing power, presence and control of the world He created.

The fact that there is no through road, means that the school is thriving with a lot of youngsters. At the time of our move, this appealed, as Margaret was pregnant with our first child Sarah. To my shame I have never had time to practically help the village, but an army of concerned hardworking capable public-minded people have willingly put in time and energy making many improvements.

Our three children have now grown up and I think they appreciate the place even more. I am grateful to God that He brought us to this particular village all these years ago. Terminally ill, I find that the graveyard is one place which has absolutely no appeal but know that the grave for a believer in Jesus is not the end. The best village in Scotland will be nothing compared to the place prepared for those with faith in Jesus as Saviour: *A city that has foundations, whose designer and builder is God* (Heb. 11:10).

Rev Alasdair Smith

I have been impressed by various people who were cured from terminal illness, here is an account of how my father-in-law, Alasdair Smith, at the age of eighteen, survived against all the odds humanly speaking.

Alasdair Smith was born prematurely in a black house in 1925, the eldest of seven. In 1944, at the age of nineteen, while serving in the Navy during the war, he was sent home to Lewis with pneumonia and pleurisy. The Lewis Castle was at that time a naval hospital. Alasdair went into a deep coma and was given absolutely no hope of recovery. The doctor even instructed his father to have him measured for a coffin. Despite being in a deep coma, he could hear all the discussion and clearly remembered the well-known Stornoway minister, Rev Kenneth MacRae, praying over him with the assumption that he would die. He also heard two nurses talking about the sadness of such a young man with no hope of life. Although angry with God, because his mother had died the previous year, he knew without any doubt that God had plans for his life. Alasdair had a crystal-clear sense of this. He would indeed go on to live a long time and have a productive Christian ministry, although that was to be some years in the future. In fact, it was a further ten years before he became a Christian!

With that clear knowledge and belief that he would survive, he was the first Lewisman to be treated with penicillin in Lewis. He was then

Rev Alasdair Smith, Murdo's father-in-law.

flown, at the inception of the air ambulance service, for further convalescence in a west coast howling storm to Aberdeen, via Kirkwall, because the weather was so bad.

Now, perhaps a sceptic could say that nothing other than the penicillin cured him. However, his strongly held conviction when he told the story, was the certain knowledge he had that he would be cured and would become a minister, despite him having no faith at that time and there being no hope given prior to his treatment. Having recently attended his funeral, where much was said about his life, I want to give you two personal memories of him.

Firstly, on discussing some of the harder theological issues, I would ask his view on some of the inexplicable aspects of Christianity. A good example would be matters surrounding the virgin birth. On some occasions, helpful discussion would follow, but sometimes he would just say, 'Well, it is just a mystery.' Many others have, in the past, fobbed me off with neat but unconvincing answers. The great Apostle Paul of course said, *'Great is the mystery of godliness'* (1 Tim. 3:16). It is possible that we will spend eternity and not fully understand everything concerning the great Creator God. Scientists today, despite remarkable discoveries and confidence, admit freely that even in the twenty-first century they still know very little about the properties of light. HOW IS JESUS EXPRESSED IN THE BIBLE? 'The light of the world!' Of course, we should grapple with these mysteries and indeed pray that the revealed Word of God would speak to us. But should we be concerned at all by our lack of theological knowledge? NO.

Secondly, we would from time to time talk of great sermons and great preachers of our day. Alasdair would agree that there are indeed many tremendous contemporary communicators, who have a great grasp of, and total confidence in the Christian gospel. He would then state that the power of the Holy Spirit is no longer behind the church in such an obvious way. This is a man who, of course, lived through times of revival and deep spiritual blessing on the Island of Lewis. Even I know that when God is at work, the atmosphere is different. His experience of extraordinary spiritual blessing was stronger, deeper, longer-lasting and wider-reaching than mine. How the church, particularly in Scotland, should pray that great days of revival and awakening would return. God has not changed.

Planes and Preaching

With a part-time lay preaching ministry all round Scotland over many years, I was aware that with the steady decade by decade increase of secularism, many small Highland churches were needing support. So, from circa 1999, I started flying to remote parts of Scotland to take church services.

Here is a typical trip to the beautiful Island of Mull. On arrival at Cumbernauld, both the flying club operators and friendly airport staff are bemused by my formal appearance: dressed in a suit, equipped with my Bible in one hand and flying case in the other. Very soon into the flight the iconic and much photographed Ben Lomond is in sight as I settle into the forty-minute journey at 115 mph with a pleasant tailwind. Even though the glorious Highland line dominates the view from my home near Stirling, I am pleased to be heading north west in the ancient 'spam can', as today's plane is nicknamed. Although I have a chart and compass, Salmond's wind farms serve the purpose of terrific navigation aids. You just have to go from one to the other, relax and enjoy the very best scenery in the world.

There is, of course, a very powerful sermon for me as I go to preach on Mull! It is the type

Murdo with Peter Morrison

of day where you just can't help but ponder the psalmist's words, *'The heavens God's glory do declare, the skies his hand-works preach'* (Psalm 19:1).[1] Consider also Psalm 36:5: *'Thy mercy, LORD, is in the heav'ns; thy truth doth reach the clouds'.*[2] The love and mercy of God is so much greater than we can ever grasp.

Very soon I am above the scenic town of Oban at 4,000 feet and resist the temptation to throttle back, because the Firth of Lorn has to be crossed and I do not fancy landing in the 'drink', as aviators call it, should the rather

The Socata TB10 which Murdo enjoyed flying

1. www.psalm-singing.org/psalms/scottish-1650

2. www.psalm-singing.org/psalms/scottish-1650

tired old single engine fail. Aware of the amazing heritage of the area, I think of Columba and his men over 1,400 years ago boldly taking the light of the gospel to Scotland; what would they have made of my flying machine?

With the airfield in the spectacular Glenforsa bay just around the corner, I radio David Howitt, the operator. 'Land on the high side,' he instructs: the side closest to the shore is boggy. Two emerging figures can be seen chasing sheep away from the grass runway. John Maclean the Elder and David are doing a vital job!

Flaps fully lowered and slowing down to sixty knots, I think of the glorious fact that should I mess up, then the important part of me – my soul – goes immediately to the nearer presence of Christ in glory! However, I have an astonishingly strong desire to live and to treat the situation with the respect it deserves. The original owner of the battered forty-year-old Cessna I am now flying, a few decades ago, landed short in the trees at Glenforsa. Although the colour scheme of the aircraft has changed since then, David had, on a previous visit, shocked me with the accident photos from his scary, rather depressing album full of Glenforsa mishaps. He tells me that despite having been a sceptic where the Christian faith is concerned, the pilot walked out of the wreckage and knelt in a prayer of thankfulness! WISE MAN. My own landing is competent enough on the forgiving soft grass and fifteen minutes later I am enjoying refreshments in John and Molly Maclean's home in Craignure.

The simple sermon at the idyllic little church draws on my own experience as a believer. As very much just a lay preacher, I cannot draw on the first class rigorous training our full-time men in the Free Church have enjoyed.

How sad though that the Christian faith is at such a low ebb in the area where the Good News was originally brought to Scotland. Despite low numbers at the service there is no greater privilege than telling people of the Saviour who died, rose again, and can save completely for time and eternity all who come to Him in faith. It beats flying, it beats any form of business or entertainment, it is truly out of this world!

Today, almost on the threshold of 2017, the church in Scotland needs to innovatively and confidently spread the Good News. Elijah, the Old Testament prophet, thought that everybody in Israel had turned from the faith to find that there was still a remnant of 7,000. One thing I have learned from the response to seventeen blog posts over the past five weeks, is that the glass is still half full in Scotland.

A Glance ... and then ...

Yes, it was just a look between Margaret and myself and Stirling Free Church was born!

Back in 2012, Rev Alasdair MacDonald had intimated that he was retiring from Dunblane Free Church in a few months. What would the congregation of thirty people do? Could we afford another minister? As is the case with so many small churches, the answer was not clear. In December 2012, I found myself presenting various options to the congregation using my first ever Powerpoint presentation. In a previous life, talks had been given using acetate sheets and a now obsolete primitive projector.

My own favoured option for some time had been to bring someone to Dunblane who could spend time establishing a new church in the city of Stirling, the local centre of population five miles away. There seemed to be strong resistance to the shared ministry idea which was expressed in the words from the floor, 'What is Stirling to us?'

We had always felt that there was a very strong case for planting a new Stirling Free Church and we found ourselves praying, particularly when travelling east on our way to Dunblane with the castle in view, that a way would open up to start a church in the city. It took twenty-four years between thinking about it, praying for it, and the birth of Stirling Free Church. With roots, friends and family in the north, Margaret and I quite often thought that we should head back there, but both had a strong sense that it would not be right.

Following a couple of Dunblane Kirk session meetings where, to my surprise, there was no objection to the idea of a new church in Stirling, I took the idea to presbytery. Despite a degree of ardent support, getting the, by now much cherished dream through presbytery was a different matter! I am sorry to say that by the time it was agreed, I had lost my temper on more than one occasion. Presbytery does not sit well with me ... perhaps a bad reflection on my character.

I ensured that a dossier of information had been prepared only to be told that I was stepping ahead too much! Despite this negative experience I am a Presbyterian by conviction, I just cannot stand the politics! To be fair to Glasgow Presbytery, a layman wanting to start a church was an unusual or even unheard of request.

Neil Macmillan, the Edinburgh-based development officer, was extremely supportive but had no money to offer. He suggested we get a core group of eight to ten committed people together and start services in our home; not ideal since we live six miles west of the city. The task seemed impossible especially because we were totally convinced that nobody should come from Dunblane Free Church. Because we'd put much time and effort into it over many years, the last thing we wanted was to see that congregation weakened in any way.

Within two months, by nothing short of a miracle, more than ten people were meeting fortnightly. God is the God of the impossible!

This was to become even more clear as the congregation developed. We live in days when two churches a week are closing as Scotland becomes increasingly secular, yet in the will of God here is a church growing and developing.

On Sunday, 30th June 2013 the first official fortnightly evening service took place in the very basic Guide Hut in Glebe Avenue and, due to overwhelming support from well-wishers, forty people attended. As, understandably, the initial interest faded, numbers settled at an average of twenty-five or so. The tremendous advantage of being part of the Free Church is that we have been able to call on very good preachers. People attending were amazed at both the consistency and the Christ-centred nature of the preaching. Over many years in the Free Church College, now ETS, there has been emphasis on quality training for ministry. The fact that we have excellent young men in ministry, makes me hopeful that the future of the faith in Scotland is not quite as gloomy as some would have us believe.

Move forward to February 2014 and we started morning and evening services at the Smith Art Gallery, a huge improvement.

Although the morning service was very poorly attended initially, by late spring 2015 we were in a position to appoint three elders, another milestone in our history. Feeling the initial effect of what turned out to be a brain tumour, I was delighted to pass on some of the duties to others. To be firmly established we needed a manse, minister and our own premises. Approaching the denomination for help in these three areas, I was fobbed off and told that we were nowhere near ready to afford a minister or manse. Within less than a year, through the help of God, we ended up with both minister and manse.

Stirling Free Church group photo

The obtaining of permanent premises is a little harder, but we do, in the opinion of many, have what it would take to secure our own place of worship. We already have rented city centre premises called 'The Well'. Many, (too many to list) ambitious programmes are, God willing, to be run from there. This will help our growth and put the Free Church on the map in Stirling.

Rev Iain MacAskill became our minister at the end of February 2016 and it is fair to say that we have doubled in size from thirty-five to seventy. His ministry has been very much appreciated by all and I believe that the God who blessed us each step of the way so far, will continue to use Stirling Free Church for His glory in the city. In this connection, your prayers would be appreciated. You will see from the text that, despite many taking the view that the task is impossible, God has helped us. We would get nowhere without His approval, power, presence and blessing.

My Biblical Garden

What is your favourite place on earth? Over the past seventeen years our garden near Stirling, for me, became in many ways a sanctuary and great foil to a fairly stressful lifestyle. I decided that having heard of and seen gardens representing human achievement, should I reach retirement age, it would be good with the help of sculptures, paths, plants etc., to create a biblical garden that would enrich groups and individuals spiritually. Here are the great truths which I would have hoped to express ...

The Garden of Eden

A perfect place with perfect people in a perfect environment. God saw that it was good and protected that amazing place. Hard to represent it, but with a bit of tidying up I reckoned it would be a good beginning to the biblical journey. As we are told in Genesis, so long as our first parents obeyed God they would live in perfect harmony with the Creator.

Banishment

Why do we die? The Bible explains that banishment then death came through sin or rebellion against God. We were originally designed to live forever. A just God would not have

Dinning House from the air

acted true to His character unless He punished our first parents. Through sin came death and I simply cannot find a better explanation for death than the one given in Genesis. My plans for this garden were to construct a sculpture of the angel described in Genesis protecting Eden from Adam and Eve. Genesis begins with the words 'In the beginning God' and ends with the words 'They laid him in a coffin in Egypt' talking of Joseph. It takes the rest of the Bible to explain how a God of love dealt with the great tragedy of death coming through sin. A number of years ago I found myself at a Bible study with an old theologian who admitted that he had previously dismissed the first book of the Bible but now recognizes the many complex layers of great and valuable meaning within that book.

They Wandered in the Wilderness

To the rear and left of the aerial photo, on page 128, there is a path between the tennis court and the trees. That is the wilderness area. There are plenty of thorns, brambles and thistles in this part of the garden (if you can call it that). These represent a fallen world and the curse of the fall of mankind on planet earth. It was no longer a perfect environment but a harsh place, a place where death had come through sin. In the second book, Exodus, we have the children of Israel wandering in the wilderness. There are many spiritual lessons to be learned by considering the dealings of God with them. I would, with my biblical garden, pretty much have left this area as it is … a challenging environment, even to walk through.

The Cattle on a Thousand Hills are His

The splendid fields and hills around the garden look superb. Who do they belong to? The Bible tells us that they belong to the great Creator Himself and a plaque looking out on the fields and hills with a text such as, *'The earth belongs unto the Lord and all that it contains'* (Psalm 24:1)[1] would have been very appropriate, perhaps with a seat nearby to give people the opportunity to contemplate the control our Maker has over the world He created.

The Solid Foundation

Is your life built on a solid base? Jesus tells us of the man who built his house on sand with

---

1. www.psalm-singing.org/psalms/scottish-1650

disastrous results. Are you certain that your life has a solid foundation? Jesus describes Himself as the way the truth and the life. Is there a better foundation? No there isn't. But let me give you an example of a very poor foundation. In the year 2000, I built a tree house for my children. It looked great with its trap door, verandah and swing! However, if you were to look at it today, you wouldn't see much. I'm astonished that even a scrap of it still stands. You see, the foundation wasn't solid. Made from scraps of wood, there is virtually nothing remaining. The exact opposite to the eternal, solid foundation of our Lord and Saviour Jesus Christ.

The Brook that Runs in the Way – Psalm 110
I have always found the prophecies of the Old Testament concerning Jesus a great re-assurance when any doubts creep in. There are hundreds of direct references to the birth, life, ministry, death and resurrection of Jesus throughout the Old Testament. Most of them unmistakable in clarity and of course proven scientifically beyond doubt to be written before the time of Jesus. My favourite in recent years has been Psalm 110 which takes us to

a conversation between God the Father and God the Son after the ascension. Those who understand ancient warfare know that for effective combat a plentiful supply of water was needed. Jesus, in dying for our sins, broke the power of the devil. Read Psalm 110 and ask the question, 'How was this account of events written 1,000 years before the death and resurrection?' The 'burn', as we call it in Scotland, runs through our garden and reminds us that the Saviour sits victorious at the right hand of God, having completed His work.

The Well

Little wonder the idea of a Bible-themed garden came to mind, when you consider all the references to wells throughout Scripture. The believer, of course, drinks from the well of salvation; the Saviour revealed Himself to the woman at the well. In our garden there is an ancient well that our children had great fun excavating. There was plenty of old pottery to be found. Tony Robinson would not have a look in when they got going! On a serious note, have you been to the well of salvation?

Therefore with joy shall ye draw water out of the wells of salvation (Isaiah 12:3).

The Straight and Narrow Way

There are only two ways – the straight and the narrow way which leads to eternal life and the broad road leading to destruction. When we first moved to the house, I established a path round the perimeter and very quickly a long narrow way through the broom was established, the lawn mower could just squeeze through. My plan for the biblical garden was to have a broad pleasant avenue alongside, representing the broad road leading to destruction. The great question is, which road are you on?

Death Vanquished

Death is described as the last enemy but for the believer Jesus on the cross conquered death. This is the lowest and most peaceful point of the garden and the idea was to have a nice seat and the text *'Teach thou us our end in mind to bear'* (Psalm 90:12).[2] I certainly need a constant reminder that we all have an

---

2. www.psalm-singing.org/psalms/scottish-1650

unavoidable appointment. It is great to have a Saviour who has defeated the last enemy.

Do you take the time to focus on Jesus Christ who vanquished death on behalf of His people?

> *For we know that if the tent that is our earthly home is destroyed, we have a building from God, a house not made with hands, eternal in the heavens* (2 Cor. 5:1 ESV).

Journey's End

There is a church next door to our home, the house of God on earth with the cross in a prominent place. For the believer, a house and even a mansion has been prepared in heaven itself!

Given my own terminal condition, the earthly house and garden will soon be for sale and if you would like to buy an amazing family home in a great part of Scotland and have the vision, time and energy to create a biblical garden, talk to me!

I have not even mentioned bridges, Latin inscriptions and pre-Christian burial sites ... The scope for something top notch, with a powerful message, is clearly just waiting to be exploited.

Marriage

There is so much talk these days of misery within marriage and failed marriages. Here I am battling terminal illness and facing premature separation from Margaret after just twenty-eight years. Having enjoyed a good marriage, this does not seem fair on either of us. Hard as it is, during ongoing terminal illness the bond is even stronger and our three grown-up children strengthen that bond and make my imminent death seem all the harder to accept in the will of God. Why us? Everything seemed so right when we got together nearly thirty years ago. For sure, within Christian circles there is more than a tacit expectation that there should be a strong sense of guidance from God prior to marriage.

At the great age of twenty-nine, as well as feeling no particular attraction to the many young women in the circles I moved in from day to day, more disturbingly for me there was a distinct lack of spiritual guidance.... that was about to change! The local Free churches had youth groups which met each Sunday evening and I was asked one evening to speak to a crowded room. The young people were the teens and twenties age group and I sensed that the meeting had gone fairly well. At the end of the talk, as we enjoyed supper, I overheard an extremely attractive young girl, who had asked both relevant and intelligent questions, tell the host that they had just heard the best speaker ever! The next few months were to prove, beyond all doubt, that a bit of flattery works every time on a man! How could I resist this girl now?

Margaret had, a few weeks earlier, spotted me in a crowd outside the Free North Church and, without knowing who I was, knew beyond all doubt that we would be married. Despite her youth, she made up for what I lacked and still lack, in direct spiritual experience. For example, one evening she observed a mysterious column of light and heard heavenly singing go up from a house in the village where her father was minister. It proved to be the death of a godly lady. Similar occurrences have not been my experience, despite my firm belief in the Bible as the Word of God, so in many ways we supplement each other very well. The last thirty years leave me in no doubt that a sovereign God brought us together.

Murdo and Margaret on their Wedding Day

Scripture makes it clear that there will be no marriage in the glorified state. However, I would like to think that we will know each other in heaven. Somehow it would seem to me unfair not to know family members and friends.

Within our marriage, it would be wrong to say that everything has been straightforward. As two very different people, there have been tensions. The differences are too complex and nuanced to put on paper, but often the differences have made us stronger as we supplement each other. This terminal illness seems so unfair, yet we both trust that God is working it for good.

Conclusion

You will have read much about faith which has been so much part of my life in this book. The vital question is, can we be sure about our faith? There have been times when all I have been able to say is that the gospel makes sense, the teaching of Jesus is amazing. According to Scripture, we have a sure and certain hope that belief will bring me to heaven. However, every believer wants more than the basics and to know something of Jesus is to want to know more! Scripture asks us to 'love not the world or the things in it'. If I were to criticise my pre-seizure life, despite being a believer, I spent far too much time on what is described in the Bible as 'temporal matters'.

Looking at your own life, let me ask you very pointedly and personally, are you neglecting spiritual matters? How much time do you spend reading the inspired Word of God? What about prayer? Are you sharing the Good News with others?

The believer has a secret weapon; God the Holy Spirit is within us. But we often pay little or no attention to that wonderful prompting, guidance and reassurance and go our own way. Since summer last year I can honestly say that I have listened more to God the Holy Spirit and

Garage in Kyle with Kyle Free Church to the right

my faith and assurance is much deeper than it was … Remarkable that it took terminal illness to deepen my trust in God. As I conclude this book in April 2017, I am at peace but also find it amazing that God had to allow a serious debilitating, distressing experience to bring me closer to Him.

Despite the various very good medical people holding out little or no hope beyond a year, I still firmly believe that if the Great Physician wants to heal me, then that is what will happen. Who knows what job He may have for me?

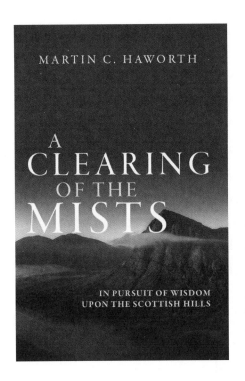

A Clearing of the Mists
by Martin C. Haworth

The mountains of Scotland have long drawn people to their rugged peaks and rolling tops. Drawn by the physical quest, the desire for solitude or for many, the deeper search for purpose and meaning in their life experience.

Martin C. Haworth was drawn to wild places, searching for that connection with something pure and great. In that search, he has known the spiritual glimpses that God communicates to us through the awe-inspiring grandeur of wild places. Join him in this devotional journey through the Scottish hills.

ISBN: 978-1-78191-718-3

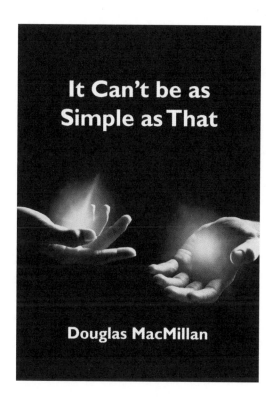

It Can't be as Simple as That
by Douglas MacMillan

Share this small but powerful booklet with your friends, share it with your family, share it with everyone who needs to know Christ. This is Douglas MacMillan's personal account of his conversion. As an atheist, he couldn't accept the simplicity of either Christianity or the Big Bang theory. When a friend held out two hands and said, "In this hand, I'll give you everything you are afraid of losing; and in this hand I'll give you Christ," Douglas realised that it was a simple choice after all.

ISBN: 978-1-78191-103-7

Christian Focus Publications

Our mission statement –

STAYING FAITHFUL
In dependence upon God we seek to impact the world through literature faithful to His infallible Word, the Bible. Our aim is to ensure that the Lord Jesus Christ is presented as the only hope to obtain forgiveness of sin, live a useful life and look forward to heaven with Him.

Our books are published in four imprints:

CHRISTIAN FOCUS

Popular works including biographies, commentaries, basic doctrine and Christian living.

CHRISTIAN HERITAGE

Books representing some of the best material from the rich heritage of the church.

MENTOR

Books written at a level suitable for Bible College and seminary students, pastors, and other serious readers. The imprint includes commentaries, doctrinal studies, examination of current issues and church history.

CF4•K

Children's books for quality Bible teaching and for all age groups: Sunday school curriculum, puzzle and activity books; personal and family devotional titles, biographies and inspirational stories – because you are never too young to know Jesus!

Christian Focus Publications Ltd,
Geanies House, Fearn, Ross-shire,
IV20 1TW, Scotland, United Kingdom.
www.christianfocus.com